COTTON AND SPIRIT

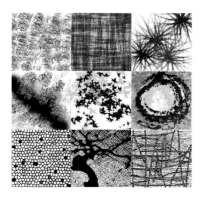

POETRY BY

KATHIE ISAAC-LUKE

ELAINE F. KAHN

JEAN LIN

NANCY L. MEYER

JUDITH OPPENHEIMER

STEPHANIE PRESSMAN

MARY ANN SAVAGE

ARIEL SMART

MARY LOU TAYLOR

BERNIS TERHUNE

PHYLLIS WILLIAMS

frog on the Moon
A small press
Cupertino, California
January, 2006

To my dear sisters in creativity
nancy

Library of Congress Cataloging-In-Publication Data
Library of Congress Control Number: 2005938733

ISBN 1-59975-468-1
  978-1-59975-468-0

Poetry

Cover art, graphic quilt squares, and book design by Stephanie Pressman
Typeset in Ehrhardt MT; printed on acid-free paper.

FIRST EDITION

QUILTING

As women before us
wove stories into fabric,
we, in a circle of language,
gather poems.
Piece together
shadows of memory.
Layer the tenuous texture of adjectives.
Stitch in the pure geometry of nouns,
the swirling pattern of adverbs.
Watch verbs
begin to push and pull
their way through our creation.

We bind truth with myth,
line it with stiff-shouldered sorrow.
Fasten on falling-down happiness; pull
the cover of poetry over us,
as our grandmothers once did
with quilts they fashioned
out of cotton and spirit.

— Jean Lin

CONTENTS

As women before us
wove stories into fabric,

WOVEN STORIES

2

BLAME APHRODITE

My daughter is in love.
I should object to this —
they are so young.
She tells me of her plans.
I see the pitfalls,
yet I can no more point them out
than I could prevent her tumble
when she scaled the slippery
bars of her enameled crib.

No matron from Jane Austen
was ever giddier,
or more conspiratorial.
I finger lacy fabrics,
plan the menu for a feast.
The fellow doesn't stand a chance.
We plot against him —
I play his advocate.
What is the source of
this newfound irrationality?
An atavistic urge
to propagate the species?
Am I reduced to genes?

My daughter charts her course.
I have no say in this.
I cannot walk her to those stars
that guide her now.
In a glow equal to her own,
I turn toward my bewildered
husband and find his eyes
remembering.

First published in *The Montserrat Review*, Fall 2001.

SYMPHONIE PATHETIQUE

After I wait all day in her skid row room, Mother
is ready at last to take me shopping.
A sophomore now, I'm obsessed with clothes
believe boys will ask me out if I wear the right sweater
that elitists will include me in, never guess the pathetic
parent I have, once I also wear the right skirt —

navy pleats stitched down over the hips, a regulation skirt
to wear Fridays for middy day like girls with mothers
who know the clothes they need and buy them, not pathetic
mothers like mine. I'm painfully aware she can't afford to shop.
Do I dare ask for both a skirt and a white angora sweater,
I with my snaggle-toothed smile, hated mirror image? Clothes

could transform me. I'll die if I don't ask, desperate to be clothed
like the in-crowd. When it's not middy day, they wear plaid skirts
with stitched down pleats, colored cardigan sweaters
worn backwards, and penny loafers. "Today, *Maman,*"
I can just hear them say, "I'm much too weary to shop."
Now isn't that a *symphonie pathetique?*

If they only knew what real pathos
felt like. How can I even think about clothes
or letting Mother take me shopping
when I know if she buys just the skirt
alone, she may not eat next week. She needs mothering
more than I do. Nevertheless, I look for the sweater

in Junior Separates at Rhodes Department store, sweat
till I find it. She tries secretly to count what's inside the pathology
of her purse. It looks run over by a truck. If I disagree with Mother's
choices, she's so fragile she might just come apart, but the clothes
she picks are all wrong. *My* choices - the sweater and navy skirt —
fit perfectly. I hate myself for what I'm about to do. No need to shop

further, though Mother still wanders, sneaks looks at prices, shops
for buys. After I put on the white, buttoned-in-back sweater
gaze in the mirror, ecstatic, I imagine my new life, skirting
reality. *Just this once,* I decide, *I refuse to be sympathetic.*
She says, "Sweetheart, are you sure these are the right clothes?"
I answer yes. She gathers the skirt fabric in a ball to test it. My mother

wavers between sweater and skirt, longs to please, but there's the pathos
of her pocketbook. When she asks a shopgirl to wrap both items of clothing
I steel my heart against the thought: *what's to become of Mother?*

GENERATIONS

Grandpa tied Johnny to a fence,
whipped him with an old rope
until he cried like a little boy,
promised, broken, he'd stay home,
work hard, not run off to town.

Life is easy on the Central Coast.
Winter is rain, and not much of it,
lots of years.   Water comes in
to the crops through pipes.
We can farm the winter, go outside.
Not like Texas, where Grandpa's pa
froze to death, and his horse too,
when he got lost in a blizzard.

Grandpa was sixteen,
Johnny's age now,
when his pa died. He
brought the family here,
worked for Mr. Matheson,
and didn't get the farm
or his wife,
or any rest to hear him tell it,
until he was thirty-two.

OFFSPRING

In another time they married,
moved around the corner
or across the street. Less often,
they moved to the new country
or the old, their steamer trunks
in tow packed with their bedding,
the careful quilts with
delicate even stitching.
And you missed them,
but adjusted to the silence.
Letters arrived with
some predictability,
and photographs you
studied until they were as
familiar as their faces.

Now, when you think you
have adjusted to their absence,
they appear unexpectedly
on your doorstep to stay,
or to leave again, taking
their belongings
or abandoning them,
your heart in a state
of suspended animation.

First published in *Muse Apprentice Guild*, Summer 2003.

CLICK CLACK

Tongues click faster
than Mahjong tiles that
clack their way across the table
like noisy crickets.

"An American girlfriend,
not such a good thing,"
Mrs. Wan observes.
She places a tile, yells, "*huh dow!*
Lots of trouble, I think."

"American style, very different than Chinese,"
adds Mrs. Chen, cracking a
watermelon seed with her teeth.
"American women cook food without taste;
the only Chinese dish
they know is chop suey."

Mrs. Pang, jade bracelets clinking
against slender wrists, frowns,
"When they get older,
they become very fat;
skinny now, yes, but fat later."

"Lots of problems,
lots of divorces in America,"
they sing out, a Chinese version
of a Greek chorus.
The tiles spin faster, faster;
the words grow louder, louder;
Peter's mother grows dizzier, dizzier.

"Ma fainted today at Mrs. Chen's,"
Peter tells me that evening.

"Maybe we should call off the wedding."

Clacking tongues,
words flung across a Mahjong table
might seal our fate.

WANTS IN A FRIENDSHIP NOT BEING MET

A land tortoise lived in our neighborhood when I was growing up.
When it came into our yard, we lifted it to take it home,
stroked its head and crooned to it, protected it from the woman next door
who screamed at it and kicked it when she found it in her yard.
I loved its cool dry head, its old eyes.
It might have been over fifty years old. Now I am.
Sometimes I don't know any more about myself than I did then.

Who is grieving here? I haven't lost that land tortoise.
It's still digging its claws into my chest, still plodding
slowly from yard to yard, over one hundred years old —
a good age for tortoises.

> *black rock composite with reds and silvers,*
> *a quartz outcropping on its neck,*
> *tortoise shaped, head and legs retracted*
> *flat on the bottom, round and dimpled on the top*
> *heavy, it drops with a thump,*
> *leaves a nest in the sand*

I give the rock to my friend. I want to ask for it back
but I want her to have it. I want to say, "This is a sacrifice
I make for our friendship." I want her to stay with me
on my terms, to have intimacy, outward expression on my terms.

I am unraveling an old sweater with a hole at the center
caught once on the claw of that tortoise. An old unraveling,
the issues the same, all of my friends at school while
I waited too young, finding the tortoise in the yard, no sounds
but my own breathing, my own heartbeat, the gentle scratching:
claws in the sandbox, thick and leathery, following its path.

SISTERHOOD

After a dozen years, an even dozen, my ex-husband came back, smack-dab out of the blue, as if he'd only been to the 7-11 for dishwasher soap. And even though my cat, the wisest of cats, who I'd named Sigmund Freud long before I knew how apropos the name would be, even though Siggy's orange fur stood up — straight up — for days, weeks on end, even though he meowed "I smell a rat!" sounding more like Freud than a cat, yowled "My theory was wrong! You only need work. Who says you need love?" as he rolled owl-like, amber eyes at the skies, *still I let that man back in.*

Then shock waves ricocheted off fences miles away. Even Siggy's ears stood at attention, his periscopic tail doubled in size! For all at once, before my very eyes, all the unfettered women I knew, had ever broken biscotti with, discussed Alice Walker with over coffee, even some I didn't know, transmuted into harpies, began to fly around the walls of my house, upstairs and down, to screech and moan in every room, soaring, sinking upon green wings. Siggy made a dive for it under the couch, peered out at what looked like a squadron of green monkeys from Oz. "Don't do this. Don't do this," they cried. "Stop, before it's too late! In the name of all that is or isn't holy, don't betray us!"

A previous version was published in *Montserrat Review*, Volume 5, 2001

SPLITTING THE DIFFERENCES

Silver becomes *sliver*
unfamiliar English syllables
tripping on
my husband's
Chinese-bred tongue.

My turn to practice.
I try *Lao Shr, old teacher;*
the words for "old shit"
stride boldly forward instead.

Chinese words bound
by my American ears;
unused to dancing discrepancies,
chiming Mandarin tones.

Words so close, yet so far apart,
a sliver of a silver moon sails
across the waiting sky;
old teachers really were
old shits sometimes.

Naughty words
were the ones
I wanted him
to teach me first
after *thank you,*
hello, I love you.

Language lessson over,
I make tea.
Earl Gray for me,
cream turning it
the soft color of caramel candy.

He takes fragrant jasmine,
amber brown like his eyes.
Reaching out for his cup
our hands touch,
splitting the differences.

BURIAL GROUND

Breaking open a Coors by eleven,
the husband dug a trench six feet deep.
His Aussie pup frolicked and barked
at foreign smells
and squirrels on the fence,
while the man leaned by his pickaxe.
Sweating, thirsty, he tilted back his neck,
burned red by ale and sun,
guzzled and pitched aluminum cans in the hole,
joining the booty of empty vodka bottles,
dead soldiers, he called them,
once quartered in the garage
under a tarpaulin tent.
Surrendered now, they lay heaped in a common grave.
In time, an army of muddy necks
popped up uniformly
after the rains.

UNDER A MIDLANDS SUN

Through shady groves
of blue oak and madrone
to bright sunlight
and a wide, barren land spotted
with thick patches of gorse.
Bare Irish land.

A mountain sheep lies, small
against the Vee beyond, lets out
not a plaintive sound but almost
a donkey's bray, again and again,
a call from the heart.
The sheep's matted head lifts
with longing toward the road.

Another sheep silhouetted on the verge
stands in a frozen minute. Suddenly
the small sheep lunges up, plunges
through the growth, on, on and up,
until it reaches the road, butts its snout
against the big sheep's backside.

Now I understand. I can name them
he and she. Such a human act. The wife
waits for her mate to come home, sits
by the fire, stands at the door. Finally
she goes in search of him, finds him,
gives him a shove toward hearth and home.

I watch the two make their way down the hill
and back toward me through the gorse.
In the lead is the ram, the ewe following
with docile step and lowered head. They turn
together and stand above me. The satisfied look
in the ewe's eyes makes me smile.

SLINGING HASH

I daydream behind the counter
before the customers arrive for breakfast special.
Now it all looks so simple, this Santa Maria del Fiore —
Brunelleschi dashes hard the brittle brain of an egg;
he cheats a little to claim his cupola,
the dome-egg enclosed shell,
the ego of the Duomo:
a simple principle mortared,
pietre serena e fortissimo,
artisan with trowel,
(of woman born from ova,
her hair netted, no doubt)
scaffolding to heaven.
More egg play —
Donato Donatello,
carrying eggs in his apron,
Eh, Filippo, Filippo,
awe-struck falls,
beholding Brunelleschi's
crucifix of our Lord,
and scrambles them.
But what of my oeuvre?
Mere spatterings? —
Mister, how do you
like your eggs,
basted, over easy?

we, in a circle of language,
gather poems.

CIRCLE OF LANGUAGE

Nancy L. Meyer

ON BOTTICELLI'S *PALLAS ATHENA AND THE CENTAUR*

Perhaps this is the same moment —
when you wisp a smile
brush a few coins
into the dry palm of the wild-haired man
pushing his mountainous
shopping cart

Athena does not look in his eyes
Half-naked Centaur cranes toward her touch

Then shame —

he flinches his horse-legs
hugs the wall

She wraps her fingers in his hair

He is at a loss   Is this a caress?

Goddess of Law and War
Botticelli paints her
whiter   taller

Which to believe?   Will she

     judge   him

               embrace him

     Both stand off-balance

THE PARABLE OF THE BLIND
Bruegel the Elder
Louvre, Paris

Eight rustics, blind as worm-tapes,
grope their way
stupidly, in single file.
Armed with cudgels, they plod,
unwary of a dooméd fate.

They plunge, lemming-like, pall mall,
into a mired ditch.
The last fellow oaf,
mouth aghast,
tumbles into his own disaster
without a hitch.

In the background, beyond this folly,
the Master composes a bucolic,
bovine community,
a village farmhouse, church and steeple,
a peasant feeding white poulets.
A kine lifts her head
and moos lowly.
Ducks swim in a clear,
unmuddied brook.

All the while, the muddle-headed
fools plunge to death, one upon another
piled,
and break their necks
in the fall.
The canal seeps into clean water,
disposing its putrefying offal.

Bernis Terhune

THE TROUBLED HEART RECEIVES AN ANSWER

She descends covered with golden feathers
rests on the busy birdfeeder
Such beauty all breathing ceases
Greedy sparrows in noisy excess
stunned to silence
Bullying finches with red tattoos
bow embarrassed
The unnamed visitor identifiable
neither by orange flame of an oriole
nor smoky wings of warblers

The melancholy poet longing
day by day for the absence
of gloomy monotony
and dreaming of a brilliant yellow bird
now lies almost blinded
in the moment before flight
of this incandescent creature
marred only
by a charred black throat

GRANDMOTHER'S LAUGH RISES UPWARD

Kneading poems,
I fold in syllables that slide like honey
from my fingertips.

The spirit of Anna,
sits, watches,
whispers instructions,

her warm Ukrainian accent
filling
in my heart.

"A pinch of wit,
not too heavy on
the handling,
light, easy."

She begins to sing
softly,
an old folksong,

words
on a sun filled ledge,

"The poem,
a slice
of peace," she says,

"Serve,
with expectation."

EVELYN GLENNIE PLAYS CHEN YI*

Crouching low in semi-dark
you make your tam-tams
rumble: at first quietly, then, roaring.
As the lights come up you stand to face us.
Raise your arms in expansive swings.
Shatter the air with beatings on the dagu,
vibraphone, marimba, Japanese
high wood-block, Peking gongs,
Chinese cymbals and tom-tom.

You give us the music with your whole body,
hear it through your feet, your skin,
your hair flying around, fair cheeks
not like a Scottish rose
but like some exotic hybrid.

Your sounds enter my eyes.
My teeth grit on them. My skin
tingles with the high chattering
notes of the xylophone, the tinkling
of the mark-tree, the sweet golden
vibration of a bowl chime.
Until *my* body hears
what my ears do not.

*Born in Scotland, Evelyn Glennie, arguably the world's greatest living percussionist, is almost totally deaf.
Chen Yi is a composer who has written several pieces for her.

THE FOUR SEASONS

A young woman begins the first notes of *Spring*.
Her hair, tousled and to her breasts, falls
forward to cover her face; she tosses it back,
her body trembling with the rush of music,
face serene in all the sway, catching
the flicker and dance of votive lights.
Heavy with strings, the orchestra looks small,
but its sounds swell the church's vault.

The violins know their parts. The bow
of each musician flashes summer lightning.
Allegro, adagio, presto, largo: music fills
the high ceiling, turns on itself like the seasons.
My back propped against a high pew. I am
transpired, racing with *Winter* to the light.

Piece together
shadows

SHADOWS

Night Walk

Throughout the night lives a dreaded secret
the silence, the time and place caress
sleepers and find them sleepwalking

Nothing the somnambulist does quiets the secret
and nothing closes the eyes to sleep
or prevents the eyes from still seeing

The hard shadow, the state of sleep
dissolves from the same nocturnal plasma

then with the passage of desperate sleep
without reason nor object
our walk echoes

the night vibrates against our misery
and sometimes we say
we are desperate to die

and who among the shadows
of the deserted streets of night

who has not visited his countenance
coming or going
and has not felt fright, anguish, mortal doubt

the fear of the vacant body
which you and untold others
could occupy

Invasion of the Body Snatchers

Celluloid dreams stick to our
skin in the damp Florida night.

Some follow us home from the
Army base theatre, then lie with

us in the enveloping dark
as the grandfather clock bongs the hours away.

Body snatchers, would they snatch *me?*
I lift the covers off my face, peek out the window.

Would I be lost in the silvery starlight?
Would anyone know I was gone?

I hear my brother's gentle snore;
if they snatch *him*, would I play tag with a phantom Gary?

I grab hold of my bride doll;
her veil scratches my cheek as

I try to push this story out of my bed; then
body snatchers surround me, whirling dervish dancers.

I'm dizzy, like spinning on our front lawn,
watching the universe turning inside out.

I wake up screaming, screaming.
My parents rush in, bleary eyed.

"Who are you? Who are you?" I yell, pushing them back.
"Where are my real parents?"

CARNIVAL

A roller coaster ride
Dropping more than it rises
Circling
Dizzying
Twisting

The ferris wheel hesitates too long at the top.
Below a frightening fairyland
Imps
Elves
Trolls

Carousel horses chase one another.
I cannot dismount
Hurrying
Racing
Galloping

The carnival moves on without me.
I cannot catch up
Alone
Desolate
Silent

TAKING A JAZZ BREAK FROM BOSTON CHILDREN'S

Escape the beeping,
bottle dripping, nurses
rustling — my grandson's tiny moans.

Drop into an old wood chair
at Ryle's Club, stroke the thick, indented glass
foaming with Sam Adams ale. Forearms
leaden on the sticky table, taking the weight
of a three-week worry.

Piano opens, light as crickets.
McCoy's shiny shoe claps time
on the floor. Bass player
links up — a look dancing
between them — his leg lithe
against the burnished lady curves. Brush
caresses the drum, sweet as a kiss.

Now they're busy.
Jump rope spinning busy. Music wide
as a wedding smile. Loud as my pain.

Piano strides in octaves
over cymbal's steady waves.
Feather fingers blow across
strings. Drum rides in on hoofbeats —

pounds around my heart.
Loud, loud anthem,
rush over the shores of my fear.
Fear the baby, the one
so long in coming, will die.
Parents ashen at the hospital bed,
humming lullabies.

Play, play those chords.
Fill me up with breathing,
beating, soaring sound.

Kathie Isaac-Luke

BY MY LAMP

This is not what I wanted.
Not this web of tubes and wires,
this barrier between us —
what I wanted was to lay my hands
cool and firm upon your skin, to find
your pain and banish it —

This is not what I wanted,
not these cavernous halls,
these doors tinged with loneliness.
What I wanted was to fill a basin
with clear water, to wipe your forehead,
wash your hands —

Not what I wanted, not this
treadmill leading from monitor
to monitor while I adjust the ebb
and flow of fluids, oil the delicate machines.

What I wanted was to draw
my chair near your bedside, smooth
my starched white skirts and stay
to offer solace through the dreamless night.

First published in *Rusk County Poetry Yearbook, 2002*

RIVER RIDE

If you are choosing noises, pick
the sound of rocks being polished
as the river flows to the sea.

The first day in the canoe
the cliffs are giant organ pipes
singing to the wind.

Like words blinking
the drip drip of the water
oozes from the granite.

Before night the river courses on
blue, bubbling.

Under the stars on a sandy beach
I muse
whose flesh is this anyway?

The flesh of the suburban sky
gray, monochromatic or
flesh free under mica speckled sky.

For me here is no longer a needle through the world

It is cradled instead
in a gentle star–studded sling .

PLAY

No one prepared me.
He was nine to my eight
he could have been twelve,
even fifteen
tall, big, broad
he didn't talk
he made noises
like an excited dog.

I was in the home of an aunt.
Who was this child
who seemed not a boy?
He jumped on me
I was terrified.
Quickly the adults
took him away.

Later my parents and aunt
tried to explain.
mongoloid
was the term used then.
He only wanted to play.

TOURETTE'S GHAZAL

Tourists hear hoarse barking, foul language, see the flip of a hand;
it's the cursing disease. Please, won't someone give him a hand.

Landscapes of rivers and streams on display at the Musee D'Orsay:
irony of placid oils contrasts the roiling at hand.

The bent old man lets out a stream of abuse, shakes his fist.
Someone on the tour, a big guy, tries to imprison his hand.

I remember touring Chillon. The Man in the Iron Mask
wiped dust off desperate longings with his manacled hands.

Uncontrolled laughs, words incomprehensible even in French.
The old man wipes saliva and snot from the back of his hand.

People in Paris always seem to take these things in stride,
think of him more like a spoiled child hitting the wall with his hand.

They shrug and walk on. M.L., you'd better plot your escape
to the restroom. Like Pontius Pilate, you'll want to wash your hands.

BONES

In Palau
I dive around, into
a sunken Japanese World War II destroyer.

Covered with clams and soft coral — orange, yellow —
the rusted hull teems with sea life
yellow, white and black butterfly fish,
purple damsel fish,
others just as colorful.

I see, touch
the depth charges,
the stern guns,
the pocked-marked, bleached white pelvis and femur
of a young Japanese sailor.

The head of the femur
still fits perfectly into the socket of the pelvis.

At Pearl Harbor, a naval launch
manned by sailors — young men and women
dressed in crisp white uniforms —
takes me to the Arizona Memorial.

At the ship
the gun tunnels, rusted, jagged,
leap from the water.

Oil, trapped in the ship's holds,
still seeps upward
casts its rainbow colors,
its stench
over the dark blue sea.

Like a Greek chorus
names of the dead
etched in black on white marble
moan from the wall.

Previously published in *cæsura*.

SOMETIMES THERE IS LIGHT BRIGHTER
THAN SUN

even on this gray grizzled Wednesday
not close enough to Friday's promise.
Sometimes there is buried treasure unearthed
within the slow one
who stumbles doing class work,
must stay after school for special help.
The university professor on the way
to a chairmanship left notes of inadequacy
regarding Maria. The prognosis was
not hopeful.   "Auditory processing problems,
short term memory loss, unable to sequence"
that which she should. Fortunately
the classroom teacher was not told
would not give up. Even on Wednesdays.
The professor had forgotten to look into
the child's sea green eyes. There
she might have known of molten
gold foaming, waiting, then seeping
onto pages to be read and warming
a mind that on this very gloomy day
could say, "I got a hundred on spelling.
Instead of just seven right. At home nobody
help. I did myself."
Sometimes there is light brighter
than sun.

— For Ms. Medina, a first year teacher

shadows of memory.

MEMORY

Nancy L. Meyer

LADY BUG, LADY BUG . . .

Doh Boo lives under the mailbox, the army green one
on the corner of Amity and Lincoln.
Every day I tell Gramma we have to go see him.

Down the saggy back porch steps to the black
path filled with cracks and crinkles.
Turn by the smoke bush with its pinky puffs
like a dandelion, but too big to blow.

Past our dirt driveway where Grampa puts cinders
to keep the Chevy from skidding. I have a purple
scar on my knee from falling on them.

There's the Rosman's house painted purply-red.
The kitchen is so dark
shadows crawl out of the cupboards.

Here's my mailbox. I crawl under.
Doh Boo is waiting for me. He stays
high up in the dark so one can see him
but me.   I tell him everything:

Wasps are buzzing in the attic. What if they
zoom into my room at night and sting me?

Daddy and Uncle Larry are far away
in TheWar. What is TheWar, Doh Boo?
I miss my Daddy. Mummy leaves me
every day to work in a fact'ry making guns.

Gramma stares at Uncle Larry's picture
in his leather pilot's jacket with the furry collar.
Her eyes get all wet and wobbly.
When grown-ups cry   it's too scary.

Doh Boo says we'll be safe
under the mailbox.

Elaine F. Kahn

THE SMELL OF WOOD AND LEATHER

I open the door
to a dark paneled entry hall
and a heady wooden smell.

A wide staircase circles to the
second floor, hesitating halfway,
where it makes a turn.

A colored octagon glass window
looks out upon the side garden.
It is night, but

I see the sun shining through,
a bright blaze of primary colors.
I am five years old again

Sunday morning, our weekly visit
to the old Victorian home
of my uncle and aunt.

My uncle sits in the big leather chair
In the music room,
Sunday papers spread on his lap.

The sun shines yellow on the walls,
the chair smells leathery,
my uncle smells of pipe tobacco.

I run into the room, his blue eyes smile,
round cheeks dimple, his bald head
a shiny pink marble ball.

I throw myself into his arms,
clasp my hands around his neck,
the paper falls from his lap.

A dark wood paneled entry hall,
a colored octagon glass window,
soft Sunday memories cling
to the smell of wood and leather.

WHEN I TASTED COLOR

A golden sunflower
began the remembering.
I lived then
for a moment
in the childhood place.

Red was the fire from a match
ashy in my mouth.

Once I swallowed
the yellow of the sun.
It flowered in me,
planting seeds.

The sharp scent of pine
or breathing in
new-mown grass rolled
green around my tongue.

Grandmother's freshly washed sheets,
pulled the taste of white
from the wringer in her basement.

Sipping ice cold water
from a Christening cup
was silver, was silver.

Brighter than any blueberry
the blue of a lake
stained my lips.

One day my mother
handed me a box,
sixty-four Crayolas.

So many choices,
so many ways to be orange.

I never tasted color again, but I know
once I swallowed the yellow of the sun.
It flowered in me, planting seeds.

BLACK JACK

The tar bubbled up
at the side of the road
after men filled potholes.
On sticky summer days,
it smeared the Queen Anne's Lace,
made little streams in the dust.
We popped pungent black bubbles
with a twig,
put a finger in,
ouch and tasted.
It was vintage aroma,
mingling on our bodies
with the sweet sweat
of childhood in summer.
Gena Oleni used to
chew it like gum.
We were barefoot
bare midriffed
in faded halter tops and shorts.
Tar on the soles of our feet,
hard to wash off,
on summer clothes
that would be too small
by autumn anyway,
tar in our hair sometimes,
and Mother would say
You've been at the tar again.

RIVER, REVISITED

"The places where water comes together
with other water...holy places."
— Raymond Carver

A river lazes past the back doors of beach houses,
clusters of them, nestled low between dunes
in a place just half an hour north of Carmel.
Shallow, unhurried, it forks around
an island of sand just before it greets the Pacific.
Birds use the island as refuge. Yesterday

gulls huddled there, a hundred or more
close together against the wind.
Brown pelicans also claim the island,
but this time they were gone, destination unknown.
Maybe they migrate to Mexico, pendulous
elastic beaks barely skimming the swells.

The river and I first met some twenty years ago.
A man I'd grown to know, architect of beach houses,
proud of his work, eager to show it, brought me there.
We were both at turning points, freed
from long marriages, both at places of departure
beyond which nothing seemed certain but uncertainty.

We walked the white sands, past new buildings
already salted silver, past beach grasses bent double
over windswept dunes, shouted our secrets above ocean's roar,
hungry to be heard, grateful to be heard.

We stopped where the river emptied, transfixed.
Wordless, watched its quiet flow, subtle ripples,
the community of birds gathered in goodbye.
Then saw it widen, overflow like spilled varnish
on the shore, deliver itself to the daunting surf,
the enormous, undiscovered sea.

A previous version published in Poetry Center San Jose's *caesura*, Fall 2001

PENTIMENTO

painted on a canvas of "The Classmate" by Czeslaw Miloscz

Walking toward him, carrying an elongated bowl
singing because it is a hot morning.

Walking through a warren of rabbit holes,
from streetlight to streetlight

in the company of nineteen low-hovering angels,
a descent into a Thomas Wolfe novel.

Walking down a long hall that reeks
of dust, knocking on a white painted door.

Walking into a room lit with sunshine
that flows through a wall of white-framed windows.

He lounges on an unmade queen-sized bed, smoking, drinking tea,
his eyes like oceans: pale irises washing

out to sea, to sky, pupils the blue-green-black
of tidal pools, his thick glasses magnifying their intensity.

Join me, he says, *a full cup. Fall into the base and worthless life.*
He is obscure, sings ungrammatical rap, laughs

in James Dean tenor riffs. This is happening
in Berkeley, California, in a hot moment.

He used to live in someone's basement
in San Francisco. A long room filled with books,

a table with a hotplate, a single bed covered with Indian cotton,
symbols of his lost loves woven into it in bright colors.

I heard he had married, drifted into some
obscure science job. He may have died in 1976.

Does the dream mean I still long for him?
Or is it a trace of garbage not wholly discarded?

One of those hoarded bits in the garage
in a storage box labeled "remembrances."

ALL THE WAY HOME

i would win the prize yes both mother
and my sister said so first prize
in the kindergarten pet parade
they were as excited as i dressed
me as jeweled gypsy in bracelets
long ropes of beads satin vest

even rouge and wine-red lips
a silk bandana wound tight
around my short straight hair
every gypsy has a crystal ball
mine a clear glass sphere
just the right size to hold

a filmy-finned tangerine fish
named cleo she spun and splashed
in a hurry-up frenzy
we rushed to meet teddy jensen
who would parade with me
as the little dutch boy in blue

teddys dog spot wore a clown collar
he remembered not to bark as he rode
in style in teddys wagon   traffic halted
as we joined the parade near jefferson
elementary   marched down the street
and across the playground

past cheering waving moms and dads
high up judges the judges did not give the prize
to me or cleo   couldnt they see
i was the best gypsy ever   cradled
i was cradled in the arms of teddy jensens father
carried sobbing all the way home

Layer the tenuous texture of adjectives.

TEXTURES

THE DANCE MASSACRE OF SPRING

The poppings of white blossoming,
plum first, apricot, pink peach,
and white again the cherry —
Unsettled in a pool of water,
wild mallards, two drakes in combat,
rival for a hen, pinned down by her nape.
Ack, she sounds for distress,
squack, she sounds for dismay, her yellow beak agape.
The swains plunder in purple sheen and complacent swagger.
From the fence springs a flash of white and gray;
uncamouflaged, a feral cat flushes out his prey.
White blossoms and pigeon feathers, a pillow fight,
harried feathers blasted every which way.

SUMMER WIND

I crave the sleep of childhood, cool and loose,
my apple tree, thick trunked, easy climbing,
easy roosting, my tree, and I talked to it,
and the wind was friendly with the smell of apples, the sound
of bees.   Sleepy — my leg drooped, I drowsed.
I saw an apple plop to soft earth, disturb the bees a moment;
the breath of the tree touched my hair.

> Forgotten because wordless,
> but there I knew something,
> I know something, I was changed.
> Did I sleep or watch, watch or sleep,
> cool and loose while the apple
> fell, the bees rose.
> Part smell, part leaf, and wind
> We all forget, we all remember
> Breathing apple breath and sleep.

Currency of summer, neither hoarded nor wasted.

AUGUST ON THE TRUCKEE

Push out, oars poised searching the river:
We three hatted wisewomen going down river
sing ancient songs, river songs: trio and round,
rondele; searching the river.
Fish speaks its name: trout or cat,
hiding from hooks. No shame in the river
under the trees; no shame in the rushes;
only the ducks searching the river.
A water dog barks; mosquito fish swim;
rocks in the rapids catch on the rim of the raft,
and we rock it and push 'til we're free.
Snorklers in the water, searching the river;
old hooks and sinkers lie in the birches;
midges and gnats fly over the water; we float
in calm shadows of pine trees and oak;
stones in the shallows scrape on the bottom; we feel
through our feet; arms pull the paddles.
Swirl through the rapids;
change sides, searching the river;
lovers on a rock in the river's center;
the raft rushes past; change sides.
Stuck on a boulder taking on water;
push off; oars catch underneath —
close the bag, protect the book — push off;
swirl loose, searching the river.
Ophelia's hair, under the water (perhaps Clementine's),
hair of all drowned women, teachers
of the river, taught by the river, flows downstream
under the surface. Words in the river, under the surface,
inside leaves, in the paddle's drip.

FALL

Be like a leaf in autumn
    when nourishment
        no longer seeps
            all the way through.
It is dry at the base of living.

      Each day, a new color,
      you could

               drop

      at any moment.

Emptiness
makes you light, giddy.

      The new color
           is really laughter --
      you could

               drop

      at any moment.

Oh, make friends
with wind today.
      If wind loves you,
      you will fly one time,
           flutter, dance,
           then, still laughing,

           fall.

Elaine F. Kahn

FLOW

One must have a mind of water
like a somnolent stream
meandering a wild meadow
to eye tangerine poppies,
lemony wild mustard.

One must listen for the whir
of the turquoise-breasted hummingbird,
a breeze riffling distant trees.

And in the quiet of a shimmering sun
flow serenely forward
unmindful of the ocean.

previously published in Poetry San José's *cæsura*, Fall, 2005

UNDERWATER CATHEDRALS

My habitat is alive with crustaceans
hidden in walls of gold
The sea massages, warms my breasts
I worship in its crystal cathedrals

I am pregnant with the blood of the ocean
lulled by its melodic strings
suspended by its moments of silence
enchanted by its oranges and yellows
awed by the patina of a barracuda

My body evaporates —
No need to struggle
the current carries me
on my journey

I peer through
filamentous gates into watery gardens
filled with statues of colorful coral
surrounded by guests dressed in indigo, yellow
who nibble, dance, cavort

Diversity, untouched beauty
is given life by the surge,
the tide, the isolation of this
as yet untouched world.

RELATIVITY

The short, fat palm tree
beside the hibiscus
near the side window
this season is the home
of the iridescent hummingbird.

It's as near to my eye
as my hand to my elbow,
as far from my life
as the evening star.

It's nest is as big as
a rather large walnut;
the eggs there are tiny,
small as the tip
of my fingernail.

Soon tiny mouths
as big as all hunger
will cry to be fed.
Soon tiny wings
fragile as moonlight
will learn to fly.

NOT LIKE WHITE ELEPHANTS

Silicon Valley's camel-colored hills, their elephant
curves and humps, begin their subtle signs of change
after scarce few days of rain. My eyes do not tire
of hill-gazing; I seize long hours for driving.
The hills are like camels, yes. With the same wrinkles
as elephants. But almost never white elephants.
Perhaps not animals at all, they are languorous
reclining nudes, one dusky-hued shape after another.

They stretch for miles on either side, from Gilroy
to Benicia, Carmel to Marin. Full breasted, abundant
with downy hair the color of live oaks that cluster
around the dark mystery of their creases. They undulate
full of grace and sweep, contrive a winter costume:
outrageous green — brighter than all imagining.

Title after Hemingway's "Hills Like White Elephants"

Previously published in *California Federation of Chaparral Poets Convention Yearbook 2002*

Elaine F. Kahn

ISLE OF THE DEAD

A murky mist lies low over the lake
black peaks climb
out of a watery depth
as if unhinged to land.

A lone rower moves a small boat
across the mottled green,
the oars dip noiselessly in
and as quietly reappear,

no droplets clinging to their blades.
The tip of a hawk's wing,
barely visible in a charcoal sky,
brushes the treetops.

The hush of silence
hangs heavy in the air.
I am cemented
to the damp earth.

Bald Eagles

Inland, golden eagles perch
on fence posts. I have counted
fifty on Rte 5 from Willits
south to the Grapevine.

Northwest coast, the bald eludes me.
I gather information on the internet,
locations of their sightings,
then travel miles to get just a glimpse
not enough for a real identification.

Others say they have seen dozens
sitting on poles at the dock
or on the tops of lone pines.

I strain my eyes to every tree,
every jutting cliff, miss the action on the ground.
I'm annoyed by crows getting in my way —
when other times I would be amused
and even answer back their squawks —
by hawks imitating soaring flight.

Occasionally what might be
an eagle in silhouette floats
across the sky, but we find no pullovers,
and other cars trail us. By the time
I focus my binoculars, it is gone
any markings a mystery.

A friend gives me a glossy picture
book, filled with intimate photos
of their nests, their young, even
the minute details of their feed.

One night a huge male comes to me,
places his eye very close to mine
so that the white feathers
appear etched as on a crystalline vase,

so that the feathers just barely
do not touch me and I cannot
feel the stiff brush of their edges, or the silkiness
of the stroke of them,

so that his eye reflects mine
reflecting his reflecting mine
reflecting his to a pinpoint
and infinity bores into him
and me simultaneously.

After that, I see them everywhere:
flying over Seattle Zoo on a visit
with my zoologist daughter
walking beaches on the Sunshine
Coast, on hemlock tips along the shore
of Sechelt Inlet. Soaring from one tree
to the other, their white heads and tails
luminous over the glittering water,
their dark wings lifting, lifting, lifting.

CLOSE YOUR EYES AND LISTEN

Breathe shallow, one sense at a time is enough.

Let the skin's messages, the itch, the small desires,

flow past, tepid water only, noted, not attended.

Close your eyes and listen. This will take awhile.

Forget time and memory, as dust on the water.

As sounds of breath fade, stretch farther, listen under.

Beneath the sparrows' twitter across the street,

ants march below the gladiolas,

there is a slow drip from a pipe somewhere.

Across town in the little plaza, someone is mowing grass.

A star you could never see in day emits a sound like tin,

and the voice of the ocean whispers secrets.

Stitch in the pure geometry of nouns,
the swirling pattern of adverbs.

SWIRLING PATTERNS

NEW ORLEANS
The city is one very long poem. — *Bob Dylan*

The city was already dying
when it was born —
sinking back into the river silt,
the soil water-logged,
the dead entombed above ground.

The Vieux Carre, the old quarter,
a faded mistress
perfumed, still charming,
her secrets poised.

A year-long preparation
for a feast — the lent and penance forgotten
except by a few who kneel to say their rosaries
in St. Louis Cathedral above Jackson Square.

Twin steeples watch over the river which
sickles past downtown streets on its way
to the gulf, the water dotted with gambling boats,
and ghosts of barges laden with sugar and chicory.

Is it any wonder that the blues took hold here,
stayed to wander through the alleys and stalk
the tourists crowded into Bourbon Street,
an under taste beneath their sips
of absinthe frappé?

In the dry, brown refuge of my private West
I miss the mystery, that eerie greenness,
the ferns, the mosses, translucent azaleas that thrive
behind the wrought iron gates along St. Charles Avenue.

1997

A Coconut Tree Behind Every House

Firm, fleshy papayas — golden bowls to feast on — near rushing rivers above Saigon. Mangoes for breakfast big as a woman's thigh, just one feeds a small family. They dangle on long ropes, enticing, easy to reach, always gathered early, for the ripe ones turn bitter no matter how tempting. Mothers — up at dawn to cook, clean, tend chickens, geese, the stolid water buffaloes — join fathers later in the fields, small ones off to school, a chunk of sea salt in each pocket to lick between bites of juicy cucumber stolen from a neighbor's yard. Students skip along earthen levees between one rice field and another, heedless of shoots that slowly turn from tender green to ripening yellow.

> balancing barefoot
> on the shaped dirt walkways —
> the churning river

IN VIENNA, ONLY PASTRY

8:30 AM:
    Hotel balcony.
    Crusty brown
    bread, silken
    butter, melon.

1:30 PM:
    Blackberry torte,
    tangy violet gelatin
    over lavender whip cream
    pressed between
    slivers
    of yellow cake.
    A sidewalk café,
    blue breezy sunshine
    at foot of The Hofburg's
    hulking gray.

6:00 PM.:
    Ochre Schonbrunn Palace,
    rows of jewel green trees
    Cappuccino in the garden
    cocoa-tinged cream

    in thick white china,
    tiny silver spoon,
    traditional glass of water.
    Schwarze Obertorte,
    chocolate creamy wedge
    enfolded in wax paper petals,
    delicate forkfuls — each
    mouthful
    tender as a song.

8:00 PM:
    basement cafe
    jazz piano, a quick salad
    before Royal Ballet.

2nd intermission:
    two truffles
    cocoa'd mounds
    under gold leaf
    and marble arches,
    gowned patrons on
    sweeping stairways.

Impossible to eat meat in Vienna.   Only waltzes, pastry   leaven
the persistent weight
of Empire.

LOS JUNCOS
Near San Jose, Costa Rica

Jorge holds a machete
but doesn't use it.
With his hands he parts
the broad leaves of elephant ears
and poor man's umbrellas
as we make our way
through the muddy path.
The mists of earthbound clouds
sink into pools on either side of us.

Here, wild impatiens reach
to their natural heights, hobnob
with vines, splash down ravines.
We have come for the stillness,
before it explodes into the spray
of saw blades, the plodding
of cattle hooves on newly leveled ground.

When I fall, it is like I am falling
for the first time. Giddy and too sure
of my footing, I slip and tumble
into worn-out leaves, crackling branches.

A humming bird zips by,
its wings a spinning wheel.
Jorge takes my hand
and holds it just long enough
to be sure I am upright.
Then, he lets go —

Ahead there is a curve in the path
and I see my daughter disappear
behind a scalloped philodendron,
leaving me behind.

First Published in *Cafe Review*, Fall 2001

UENO PARK

You must go before the June rains.
Before latticed branches shake
their black habits.

Before pink confusion floats
like rosy snow
into a flush of petals below.

Go before thunder shakes the hills.
Before wild storms
batter spring away.

OSAKA UNDERGROUND

What I worry about most are my glasses.
Not whether Masato will meet us at Kansai Airport.
Not whether I can swallow eel and octopus or anything still moving
at one of the look-alike sushi restaurants in downtown Osaka.
Or whether I can make myself understood by the men we meet
without my own business card and only a smidgen of Japanese.

I can smile. I can listen and translate enough to get along.
Incline my head just a bit, follow obediently
in my husband's footsteps.
But my glasses are going, the frame spindly and crooked,
the lens too close to my left eye.
They'll break; then what?

I could follow the rough tiles in the train station, put there
for the sightless, like the china pattern sold in England
called Blind Earl. Fingers can trace its intricate raised pattern
until those without sight can almost see its delicate colors.
I could grope my way along, a mole wedging my uncertain way
not far below the hubbub of Japanese street life.
I could live forever in Osaka underground.

Watch verbs
begin to push and pull
their way through our creation.

PUSH AND PULL

Elaine F. Kahn

GREY

My mother's grey hair wound into a French knot
at the nape of her neck,
grey of her face in her last illness,
my own hair in the mirror,
grey shadows between daylight and nightfall,
soft, soothing carrying the repose of sleep,
calmness of a quiet evening,
giddy grey energy of daylight
chasing the night,
awakening grey of the morning,
sky grey heavy before a snowstorm
that whispers along my skin,
deep grey of the ocean on a rainy afternoon
rising in swells,
muddy grey of wet sand
clinging between my toes,
encircling grey of gulls,
cooing doves,
soft as a piece of satin,
smooth on my shoulders,
murky grey of a clouded sky,
blue grey of a sunny day,
sad grey of departure
of the song of lamentation,
the grey shadow of doom on white stucco walls,
white folding into grey
deepening to charcoal
lost in the emptiness of black.

BRAGGING
(for two voices with loud sound effect)

Tell the teacher I'm going to see my dad
Tell the teacher I'm going to see my dad

He don't have no dad to see
He don't have no dad to see

Sometimes I got no dad to see
But today I think he be coming out
Sometimes I got no dad to see
But today I think he be coming out

Jailbird, jailbird won't stay out
Jailbird, jailbird won't stay out

Today I know I'll see my dad
Or maybe he come next week
Today I know I'll see my dad
Or maybe he come next week

He had to go back, go back, go back
He got no daddy to see
He had to go back, go back, go back
He got no daddy to see

My momma she got me a brand new dad
Gives me a lot of stuff
See this brand new shirt I got
Red,   red red red

There ain't no red allowed at school
There ain't [SOUND EFFECT]
Don't matter he already dead

IN AN OLD FOLKS' HOME

If Madam did not live in a condominium,
were she free of carcinoma,
if she did not fret over a leisure calendar
and corseted diet,
nor care to budge
from Quiche Lorraine, bridge luncheons,
and widows in smocks of camellia brocade,

you would find her tucked in muslin
at Hazeldale Manor —
palsied, heart fibrillating
between tics of tic douloureux,
her mouth agape, thistle-white hair askew.
an old-fashioned face, poke-bonneted,
dreaming athwart a prairie schooner.

MINDSWEEPER

A barren woman enters a field knowing
she will be blown to bits.
Her mother gathers the pieces in her apron,
scatters them in the shadow of her 5-year-old's
grave, mingles them with her husband's dust.
At ninety-eight, willing them to her last remaining child,
she wanders through streets of memory
as empty as Herculaneum, over surfaces porous as isinglass.
Ruined walls bear fragments of faded paintings: formal parties,
celebrations, family portraits. Halls echo with a guitar's
solitary strumming. Until
the last string breaks.

TIME

Once it seemed days stood still
when I was small.
Now time slips through my hands
as age creeps up.

When I was small
birthdays were too far away.
As age creeps up
days escape in headlong rush.

Birthdays were too far away,
summer's schoolless days too few.
Days escape in headlong rush
too much to do and too few days.

Summer schoolless days too few
for games, for play, for writing poetry.
Too much to do and too few days
Years pass as quickly as a day.

For games, for play, for writing poetry
now time slips through my hands
years pass as quickly as a day.
Once it seemed days stood still.

MEMORY

Parcel out your instants.
Divide them into
easily handled units.
Store them in your freezer.
When desired, unwrap
and let them melt into mirrored
puddles — a tete-a-tete with
a handsome man in dark lenses
who sat next to you on the train
all the way through Poland —
your first drive into snow.
Some of these may be so loaded
you will need to splice them
into smaller portions.
They can be refrozen.

Nancy L. Meyer

IN THE GROUND, QUIET

Birds
thud
into our windows, often hard enough
to tremble a vase.   Usually they die
but sometimes
a stunned jay
shakes herself awake — after long moments
dead-still on the ground,
blank eye staring —
     She hops and flaps
away to an opaque branch,
a hospice of dark foliage.

My Uncle Larry has hit his last pane.
No more flapping up with jolts of chemo.
He lies still
on tight hospital sheets
          hazy-eyed with morphine.

I hope he dreams   he's floating

               in a feathered body

          floating down   to a favorite ground

perhaps

his own
          loamy Connecticut Valley land,

his tender   tended garden

                    where he can

breathe in   the tangy stems

   of the season's last tomato plants.

Bernis Terhune

"TOMORROW I MAY BE FAR AWAY"

with broken bird who wants to sing
crouching inside my chest
She takes a little hop to fly
but stumbles stumbles
rests her head on my heart
her half breaths like crying
eyes closing
eyes opening
One wing reaches out
scratches goodbye
I stay still as a corpse
My heart ceases
There is no more need
to race towards salvation

We already are far away
finding tomorrow

Quotation by Romare Bearden, painter

Stephanie Pressman

HORIZONTAL TREE
oil painting by Piet Mondrian

blue-gray ground
dark blue chiseling — vertical
horizontal — an early
Mondrian before the crisp
lines and spaces that always lead
me to rest

swirls of cerulean
rose madder strongly arch
into a trunk then fly
outward to edges
that disappear

color more faint
like the second pressing
of a monoprint
lifts into sky
blends clouds, tree, wind

but the eye is drawn
to — the heart yearns
for — the center
where paint concentrates
like sap in the pith

A steel tree stands in the courtyard
of Doheny Synagogue in Budapest
as if wire branches could anchor
the souls that holocausts
have scattered

A Douglas fir grows
in Olympic National Forest
where I wailed for loved ones
clutching its gritty bark
so I would not burst apart

WORM SONG
For my mother

How I strained
to be like her,
bold as a flagpole
flashing banners in the wind.

Instead I sing worm song.
My heart beds down in darkness,
midst the sweet rot
of leaves and unseen alchemy.

I sing of slow blind burrowing
through layers of sorrow,
tunneling in the dark,
close to wounds.

She tears back hushed curtains,
shines into corners. With searing
words, she scours tangled fields
of injustice, sends cockroaches scurrying.

I turn the salty drench of blood —
blood of wars and placentas —
into soil black and fertile as silk.   Wait
as lush little seedlings   push to the light.

She proclaims from the podium.
I hold my ear to ancient chants that roll
through the ground. We two are call
and response, call and response. Strum under all.

We bind truth with myth,
line it with stiff-shouldered sorrow.

BINDING TRUTH

Bernis Terhune

Grieving on a New Moon, June 17, 2004

(When Reagan was President, he instigated the training and supplying of a military junta in El Salvador. As a result, 70,000 Salvadoreans, mostly peasant families, were killed. There is no current estimate of killed Iraqi.)

How much sky measures 70,000 star holes in sooty darkness?
First make tight fists.
Next use them as eye tunnels.
Squint.
Count by ten thousands.

For counting
daylight is better
in the wind
by an oak tree.
On windy days my oak tree cries leaves and leaves
hundreds.
Sometimes more.

On Sunday someone ran over one of my squirrels.
Squashed it flat
under my oak tree.
A pretty one with a white belly, caramel back.
I didn't look to see if it was nursing.
The crows came on Tuesday for the eyes.
It took three days for the city to send the deads' truck.

On Being Asked If I'd Like Hasenpfeffer
At Schroeder's German Café

I'll tell you about Hasenpfeffer.
Are you thinking of Dürer's brown hare
          alert in grass, or Andrew Wyeth's hanging
                    still-life?

These on the menu were not caught in a gin.
They came hutch-tendered, petted and fondled,
          lisped by name;
Out Circe and Pinky and Daphne;
Butchery's the game.
                    Cudgel, stun, hang.
                    Quick drawn,
                    their throats throb, death scream,
                    lung wine.

Slicker pelt from flesh,
white sac at your feet.

Are the eyes pink glass buttons?
No, no.
Not Hasenpfeffer,

          Glazed.

* Hasenpfeffer is a marinated rabbit. [editor's note: a German rabbit stew]

In Taxco

The bar crowded with men standing against the walls, smoke rising from a hundred cigarettes, the men talking and laughing about what happened that day, how the police could hold them by the jugular in this Great System they lived in. Thoughts are free, not actions. The men, impatient for the main attraction, clap their hands until the girl appears wearing a bra and gauzy skirt. Full of tapas, steeped in drink, the men nudge each other, call out to her just as men do as far away as Amsterdam. The girl, so young, removes her skirt to the catcalls filling the room. This is her premier appearance. Others, too old now, have done this for long years before, the men oblivious, uncaring as to how young the child might be when she begins. I feel as if my back is to the wall. I want to thrust my way through the crowd, take her hand, lead her away. Instead, I turn my head. The girl is on the floor now. The men move forward, the whole room echoing their cheers as they watch her writhe. When the raid commences, sly old men know the back way out. *Jovenes* and the little girl disappear into the police wagon. We had just left — no place else to look but a view of the men's open urinal. Ashamed, rueful, curious, we stand outside and watch.

FAMINE

The smaller children do not know they are dying, starving. Their hunger is a state of being, always there, even after one is lucky enough to eat something. Some of them can still smile a little, and of course the mothers, too dry for tears, don't tell them. They don't say, You are dying my little one, my little prayer. They say, Things will be better soon, not adding, in another world. They say, Here, play with this rat's tail, this pretty stone. They sit, wisps of arms around wisps of children. They wait, watch the last breath, close the lovely eyes. Sometimes, too sad to stay, they move away from the stiffening torso, which is too heavy to carry to a better resting spot. Goodbye is hardly a whisper, the child is nameless now. Sometimes, it's the mother who closes her own eyes first and becomes cold. Sometimes the child moves away from a cold breast or cries a bit before he too is gone.

DIAS DE LOS MUERTOS

Under gray Mexican skies
in the courtyard of an eighteenth century stone church
a scene from Dias de los Muertos:
a mother and child in tattered clothes
huddled on a bench;
a hunched-over old man
sitting on a low wall talks to himself,
speaks in a language of his own reality.

A young man, his emaciated body
covered by an immense black coat,
shakes a small tamborine.
His skeleton arm and hand
thrust his tin cup toward me.
In the courtyard, I stride
past these ghosts to enter the church.
I expect to find colored light streaming
through stained glass windows.
Instead the plain glass yields
only a dull light.
Not even candles placed at the altar
can brighten the scene.
I will myself not to think about
the conquistadors,
the hanging trees, the brandings,
the cardinals with their blood red robes,
their death hats.
I will forget the ravages of measles, chickenpox, syphilis.
I will continue to walk, to eat sumptuous meals.

CALL TO PRAYER

Someone is whispering in her ear, tender sultry voice —
a woman singing, low tones that lure, blur into dream.
She floats in the sound — a prenatal sea
slides in the door.
Slow silken laps draw her from tight-jawed sleep —
slip the tangle of her dream.
Not a woman — a tenor — so pianissimo her bones resonate.

A microphone echoes his voice through the bowl of night.
She frees both ears from the muffle of her pillow. It must be
the mosque below her hotel window. The *muezzin* propels
the arc of prayer to every sleeping ear — whether

shivering on rags or puffed high on eiderdown.
It descends like mist on women who ignite
charcoal with stiff fingers, on children shuffling
to fill plastic buckets at a crumbling fountain, on men
who push old bones off the floor to load the donkey

Now the beat claps, the call crescendos.
Other muezzins join in — syncopated —
from scores of mosques, counterpoint
to the penetrating tenor. Chants command,
rouse the faithful for adhan.

Al——lahhhhhhhh Ak——barrrrrrrrr
She wants to take the sound home
to her silent suburb,
rise each morning from the crevice
of her lone dream to this communal tuning.
Lavender quiver of dawn mingles with song.
She glides beyond the sliver of self.

WASHTUB WITH SISTERS

Gray, slightly dented
Plump and hug rounded
Big enough for soaking linen napkins, tablecloths, sheets
        (Well, she ain't pregnant. That's for sure. . .
        Why DON'T he wash them feet!)

Depth for fishing in dark waters under suds, bubbles
        (Gimme that paddle.)

For the smaller consequents of living.
        (That boy tore up those britches. Just
        like last week.)

Heavy duty no matter how overloaded.
        (They got to pay more. I ain't no mule.)

Not fazed by wood stove scalding water
Or cruel-yellow lye soap acrid scented.
        (I got to sit a minute. You're a quitter.
        Am not! Shut up!)

Finally clanged, banged, sloppy rinsed
Prepared for washday next week.
        (Be careful! Don't spill on me.
        Cleanliness is next . . . You're going to
        get slapped!)

Rusty scratches tell of hard use
By the swollen, scarred hands
Of two fat, sweating washerwomen.
        (Hurry up. We got to get these
        things hung up quick. It's late.)

The washtub dries in the sun while
Abused hands then, now, in the future
Are mapped with deep, wide rivers
Of blood and raw pink hurt.
        (I ain't coming back next week. Me neither.)

APHORISM

When the pupil is ready
the teacher will appear,
dressed in robes embossed
with suns and moons
or wearing boots and denim,
the congruence will be clear.

Then lessons once hidden
become illuminated
as though you lifted
a single oak leaf to light
and noticed for the first time
how the central veins branched
into a mosaic of finer ones,
imprinting on each petal
the outline of another tree.

Fasten on falling-down happiness; pull
the cover of poetry over us,

FALLING–DOWN HAPPINESS

On Revisiting Uncle Les's Ruined Barn

Is making love in the loft

of Uncle Les's barn better

as we imagine it in our middle years

or as it was in youth —

weeds growing through wanton boards,

skunk smell,

the sting of weedy hay,

our toes braced against a lift.

Previously published in *cæsura*.

DANCING TO MY MASK

At one with
Athena,
Persephone and Demeter
a Mayan priestess
a Chinese princess
I dance inside a circle of women

For you the women of my world
For you the woman of my desires
I strut in my green brocaded silk robe
my golden dress.
I raise my arms to the sky
From my hands flow gold and silver threads.

I gently hold a pomegranate in my pale hands.
As I gaze at its shiny red surface
the circle of womankind shines back.
As the luscious red fruit ages, cracks
brilliant red juice becomes my life's river
spreads its fertile seeds.

My sacred circle expands to infinity.

ROMA SINGS

She performs at Lou's Club on Fridays,
billed as Brazen Hussy, a big blond woman,
larger than life, than fashionable.
Calypso Flame polish
gleams in front of gold sandals,
on fingers wrapped around the mike,
which touch Calypso Sunburst lips
or lightly brush
through the glittered, platinum curls.
Every man feels those fingertips,
every eye follows the dress,
shimmering silver, gold and black.
Her lips wake memory of a coveted
longed-for kiss under humid,
starry skies.
Sweet perspiration,
hard, expensive liquor
and White Shoulders, the scent
of another decade --
the whole room fills with lust.
Even the bartender,
towel forgotten in his damp hand,
rides the wind of desire.
This is not song, merely,
not singer merely, or even moment.
The whole enigma of Woman
sways there in the small spotlight,
breathes Yes,
breathes Maybe.

JIMMY SMITS, FRESH FROM NYPD BLUE

I want to sleep again my Jimmy Smits dream
that sweet meeting-on-the-sidewalk dream
that blind-wandering-crowds-bumbling-past-us
in-the-middle-of-Fifth-Avenue dream.

Jimmy Smits, fresh from *NYPD Blue*
except that he is eight feet tall and lifts me
up there with him in the clouds. Our eyes meet.
My legs wrap round. Heaven!

Lush, low-down, the sound of his voice
when I ask him what it's like
living so high up. "It's nice," he says
and smiles in that quiet way he has, as if

he knows some secret no one else does.
Next he looks at me all serious again.
"All day long, *querida*," he says,
"I've been remembering

how you kissed me last night."
I kiss him again, try to bring it back.
He tastes like soft ice cream
only warmer. Marshmallow syrup.

Crowds surge past, but we stay lost
in the soft, wet sweet. We float
Jimmy and I, coast in the cotton
of our Hollywood clouds. Then

he lowers me, gently, slowly like
I'm some fragile crystal goblet.
We hold hands, walk to the park
find a bench half in sun, half out.

Previously published in *California Federation of Chaparral Poets March 2002 Newsletter*

CROSSWORD PUZZLE

The woman next to me
is hunting words
to fill in nice neat squares
L
   O
      P
         S
           I
              D
                E
                  D
D
O
W
N
             SIDEWAYS

'HER' words don't   slop over
like a wet kiss
or run down my cheeks
like goodbye does
when you leave
not saying if ever
you'll come back.
I'm sick of missing you
and not saying
I love your arms about me.

  Tonight I'm drawing
    between my breasts
      with your ballpoint pen
        lines like prison bars
          with your name inside
            and putting candle wax
              on top so by midnight
                you'll call. Say,
     "I'm coming
            b
            a
            c
            k!"

The Soft, Dark Night

In the profound and humble night
your hand trembles
your face golden, white
reflects the first light of day.

The grandeur of earth's night fades.

Our reverie ends to reveal the green trees
the red tiled roofs
to hear the vendor, desperate to sell his wares
cry out.

A child, not calmed by her mother's arms,
cries beneath our window.

Traffic screeches
forms an ominous drumbeat
for the day to dance to.

To diminish the day I close
the window, the velvet drapes
We continue the soft, dark night.

THE FAN

(for Peter, Traveling in China)
after the poetess Li Ch'ing Chao

I fold
the thought of you
into my heart
again,
and again,
like a child
who delights
in her creation,

a crude paper fan
she creases
and creases
until satisfied.

Then with a wave
a cooling breeze
soothes the sun away,
tickling her chin
as she giggles into
a paper wind.

So I, too,
fold into myself
the hope of
your return
after an endless
summer drought.

I need your laugh
to bring the kiss
of a sweet autumn night
to my fevered cheeks.

THIRST

We met on Sundays, truants from the habit of church, first leaving our respective families there — his wife, my husband, our fresh-faced, starched and pressed progeny — handed them, as offering coin, excuses that were, miraculously, accepted. Aware of the irony, the sacrilege, still we flew from the Sunday sameness, decades of dark sermons. We'd fly to each other, steal time near ruins of an old villa, beside a crumbling pond. In this secret world, unbelievably close to home-school-freeway, yet so apart, so full of grace, our intent was nothing more than to be heard, seen — finally and at last *to be seen* — as separate from roles we sleepwalked through, days of mechanical giving. Around us quiet, the ruins, vineyards that survived the parched California adobe. Around us buzzing, dusty honeybees. Our communion wine a brew made from adoring words, grapes ripe with wonder. We thirsted for more, an endless supply, bathed in the delight of it.

as our grandmothers once did
with quilts they fashioned
out of cotton and spirit.

ABOUT THE AUTHORS

Kathie Isaac-Luke has a Master's Degree in nursing. During her work in that field, she visited a number of countries outside the U.S. Her poetry reflects her Louisiana origins and her travels. It has appeared in several journals, including *The Café Review, The Montserrat Review, The Sarasota Review of Poetry,* and *Reed,* and in the anthology *The Breath of Parted Lips: Voices from Frost Place, Vol. II.* She has one daughter who proofreads her work. For nearly five years she worked tirelessly as Director of Poetry San José and edited its journal, *cæsura.* She and her husband now live in Sonora, California.

Elaine F. Kahn says, "When I was a small child my mother read poetry to me, and I decided I, too, could write poetry. When I was about nine I had poetry and little stories published on the Kiddie Page of the *Brooklyn Daily Eagle.* I continued to write all through high school and college, serving on school newspapers and magazines. Out of college and in the business world, a single woman, I dropped my writing. When I moved to California, I went to San José State, earned an education degree, and taught elementary school for twenty years. At about that time I started taking creative writing classes and have had several stories published in romance magazines and articles in travel publications. A group novel, Companion Pieces, will come out in 2006. I have had poems published in *The Montserrat Review* and *cæsura.* I live in San José with my husband. We are both retired."

Jean Lin has been an educator for many years, teaching at all levels from Pre-School to University. She has contributed poetry to *cæsura, Cardinal, Rusk County Poetry Society Yearbook,* and other presses. She has completed a poetry-memoir, *Breathing Rice,* and is currently at work on a chapbook, *Pockets of Light.* She lives in Saratoga, California, with her ultra-supportive husband, Peter, and their sweet-sour cat, Jazz. She is blessed by her children, Jenny and Jeremy, and her son-in-law, Jamie. Her poems in *Cotton and Spirit* are in honor of her mother, Marian, and in memory of her grandmothers, Anna and Eliza, with much love.

Nancy L. Meyer began writing in her fifties inspired in particular by poet friend April Eiler and courses with Phyllis Koestenbaum. With no formal background in Literature, she writes to remind herself of the power to face a blank page, to hang in until you know what matters, to begin again. This also drives her passion for leading groups of women in the Journeying Home retreats she founded in 1990 and a three-year program, Women's Leadership Collaboration/west. Active grandmother of four, avid cyclist and world traveler, trustee on boards of several arts organizations, Nancy is thankful for her supportive family and busy life. Four of her poems are printed in *Double Exposure,* a workshop anthology edited by Rachel Levitsky; one poem received an Honorable Mention from the Rusk County Poetry Society in Texas.

JUDITH OPPENHEIMER is a retired pediatrician. She found her creative self during her first poetry class in 1982 and has been writing poetry ever since. Her poems have been published in *cæsura.* At the present time she is also working on her memoir. She lives in San José, CA with her son, a dog and two cats. The poems in this volume are dedicated to her son, Neal, and her brother, Michael.

STEPHANIE PRESSMAN: I started writing poetry at about age nine and finished a romantic novelette at thirteen. I have written poetry through college; while teaching high school; in between raising kids, getting an MA in English at San José State University, and teaching writing at the community college level; and during my career as graphic artist and owner of my own design and publishing business. I currently live in Cupertino, California, with my husband, one of my three adult offspring and six cats. My work has appeared in *The Montserrat Review, cæsura, Bridges, CQ/California State Poetry Quarterly, The MacGuffin, The Kerf,* and other small press magazines. I have served as a co-editor of *americas review* and *cæsura,* the journal of Poetry Center San José. As a graphic designer, I have created covers and/or layouts of several poetry books for the small publishing company, Jacaranda Press; for *americas review*; and for *cæsura.*

MARY ANN SAVAGE is a California-based poet who grew up in Appalachia. She finds the city exciting, the suburbs enlightening, and the country home-like. She loves the ocean, enjoys the wind, has learned to love fog for the layered feeling it gives to experience. She's been writing for much of her life, very seriously the last few years. She has worked in the mental health and education fields, enjoys trivia, sudoku and logic puzzles, and loves to read.

ARIEL SMART loves teaching and writing and is progressing in both endeavors. She loves being a student of literature and the humanities and is progressing pretty well. She loves a talent for friendship, a talent more than riches. She thanks her teachers Mary Jane Moffat and Naomi Clark and her husband Gordon Smart and the Peerless Poets of weekly meetings She has published two volumes of short stories with Daniel and Daniel (Santa Barbara). The *Green Lantern and Other Stories,* 1998, and *Stolen Moments and Other Stories,* 2003.

BERNIS TERHUNE, originally from Alabama, began writing plays when nine years old, inspired by a California neighbor named Eugene O'Neil. Poetry emerged later under the influence of Frances Mayes and other nefarious poets. Bernis taught special education students for many years using puppetry and creative dramatics while a founding member of a playwright's theater in San Francisco. She currently lives with her significant other, Scotland, a pound dog of mysterious origins, who cannot hear but reads lips.

MARY LOU TAYLOR's poetry book *The Fringes of Hollywood* was published in December, 2002, by Jacaranda Press, San José, CA. Her poems have appeared in *The Montserrat Review, Bellowing Ark, Tundra, Chiyo's Corner, cæsura, Reed Magazine* and other small presses. From 1982 to 2005 she was a member of the board of directors of Poetry Center San José, serving as president for two separate terms. Currently on the Lucas Artists Programs Committee at Montalvo in Saratoga, California, she also serves on the board of the Center for Literary Arts at San José State University and is a colleague of the Dr. Martin Luther King, Jr. Library Leadership Council. Her new manuscript entitled *High Music* has just been completed.

PHYLLIS WILLIAMS: When I'm not lost in the serious business of writing poetry and memoir, I continue the private practice I began as a marriage and family therapist twenty four years ago. Before that the teaching of high school and community college writing and literature, with masters degrees from Santa Clara University and San Jose State. My work has appeared in *The Montserrat Review, cæsura, Finding What You Didn't Lose, Ruby-throated Hummingbird. The Journal of Poetry Therapy* and other publications. More than three dozen of my poems have won contest prizes. In 2004 I completed two books: *Salt Years*, a poem-memoir about growing up in a family torn apart by the Great Depression, and *Sand Trails*, a collection. Since then all my energies have been devoted to moving, after nearly fifty years, from California's Santa Clara Valley back to my birthplace, the Pacific Northwest. The readjustment period seems endless. I dedicate my poems in *Cotton and Spirit* to Peerless Poets who continue to amaze me with their warmth, support and validation.